ghazals

of

ghalib

translated and
arranged by
Sasha Newborn

BANDANNA BOOKS   2012   SANTA BARBARA

SHAKESPEARE FOR DIRECTORS, PRODUCERS, ACTORS, WANNABEES

---

shakespeareplaybook.com

SHAKESPEARE DIRECTOR'S PLAYBOOK SERIES (scene-by-scene storyboarding, auditions, staging diagrams, budget, publicity, costuming, set design, playbill, stage managing)

Hamlet   The Merchant of Venice   Twelfth Night   Taming of the Shrew
A Midsummer Night's Dream   Romeo and Juliet   As You Like It   Richard III
Henry V   Much Ado About Nothing   Macbeth   Othello

plus a Shakespeare anthology:
SEVEN PLAYS with Transgender Characters, plus Hamlet

TWOHOURREADS.COM

Don't Panic: The Procrastinator's Guide to Writing an Effective Term
Paper. Steven Posusta
The First Detective: 3 Stories, Poe   Gandhi on the *Bhagavad Gita*
The Everlasting Gospel, William Blake   Italian for Opera Lovers.
Dante & His Circle. Vita Nuova   Ghazals of Ghalib.
The Gospel According to Tolstoy, Hadji Murad, a Chechen "Dzhigít"

TWO-DAY READS

Mitos y Leyendas/Myths and Legends of Mexico. Bilingual
The Beechers Through the 19th Century
Frankenstein, Mary Shelley   **Aurora Leigh**, Elizabeth Barrett Browning

---

TEACHING SUPPLEMENTS

Areopagitica John Milton   **Apology of Socrates, & The Crito** Plato
Leaves of Grass, Walt Whitman   **Sappho, The Poems**
Uncle Tom's Cabin, Harriet Beecher Stowe

CONTENTS

to a soul that speaks

INTRODUCTION

GHALIB's family traced its ancestry back hundreds of years among the Seljuk Turks, whose fortunes rose and waned and rose again. In the mid-eighteenth century, his grandfather emigrated in like a medieval knight from Samarkand to the dying Mughal Empire—as a nobleman with fifty fighting men—and he received an estate large enough to support his troops in exchange for his fealty. Ghalib's father and uncle followed similar military careers, supplying their own troops for various Indian Nawabs and Rajahs.

His father married well in Agra society, and on December 27, 1797, Mirza Asadullah Khan—Ghalib—was born. This precocious child grew up in a feudal household: one's station in life was determined by ancestry, nobility, social standing, and court intrigues. He early tasted the pleasures of the well-born. Unfortunately, Ghalib's father was killed in combat when he was four, and he was sent to live in his uncle's household.

The very next year, the British defeated the Mughal Empire, but allowed the Mughal king and his court to run internal affairs under the British Raj. In fact, the Mughal defeat marks Delhi's resurgence as a center of Islamic culture. A long-running decline had reduced a city of two million to 200,000, with whole areas ruined and deserted. The British suppressed lawlessness, and for the next fifty years, Delhi and the Mughal court attracted scholars, poets and artists from other parts of India. Delhi College was established, and both Islamic and English classics were emphasized.

At age nine, Ghalib wrote his first Urdu verse. In the same year, his uncle died, and Ghalib's life was again in turmoil. At thirteen, he was married to an eleven-year-old bride from a prominent Delhi family, and he moved in with them. His in-laws regarded him as an upstart intruder, and he spent much of his life justifying his worth to others and to himself. The protection of his father-in-law had its costs. He continued his literary studies with his Persian tutor.

Early in manhood, Ghalib rejected Urdu verse to devote himself to the Persian language, and, with few exceptions, he wrote in Persian for the next thirty years. He regarded Persian as a superior literary language, suitable for his ambition: "To polish the mirror and show in it the face of meaning—this ... is a mighty work."

Then, in 1826, his personal life suffered several blows: his only brother Yusuf went mad, and his father-in-law died. Ghalib's share of the substantial inheritance came into question because of a long and bitter dispute between two sons of his father-in-law, born of different mothers. Most of Ghalib's life was a struggle for an income; he employed his poetic skills at various courts, and he indulged in other aristocratic pursuits.

In middle age, Ghalib was arrested on a gambling charge, and in 1847, he was imprisoned for running a gaming house. After his release, he was welcomed at court—as he had long wished to be. A little later, he resumed writing in Urdu. His ghazals gained a reputation at mushairas, or poetry contests, for erudition, though some called it obscurantism.

Ghalib fared well in the 1850s, and he adopted the sons of his wife's nephew. In 1854, he received adequate stipends and court appointments. He had become a true Delhian, a respected figure in a great cultural center.

Yet in the midst of this prosperity, Ghalib saw the political weakness of Indians in their own country. To keep one step ahead, he wrote a Persian ode to Queen Victoria, with this note attached:

6

The emperors of Rum and of Persia, and other conquering kings, had been accustomed to bestow all manner of bounties on their poets and panegyrists. They would fill a poet's mouth with pearls, or weigh him in gold, or grant him villages in fief or open the door of their treasuries to shower wealth upon him. And so your poet and panegyrist seeks a title bestowed by the imperial tongue, and a robe of honour conferred by the imperial command, and a crust of bread from the imperial table.

What could not be foreseen was the Sepoy Mutiny of 1857—showing the fragility of the British hold on the subcontinent. For four months, rebels took and held Delhi, killing all British inhabitants. Ghalib closed his door and occupied himself with writing Dastambu, a diary of those troubled times. This account was generous to the British; Ghalib intended it to reestablish his career in a new era. The book was published in 1858, and amnesty came soon after.

Ghalib's friend Hali reports this story: After the British retook Delhi, a certain Colonel Burn asked Ghalib "Well? You Muslim?" "Half," said Ghalib. "What does that mean?" asked the Colonel. "I drink wine, but I don't eat pork." In Dastambu, Ghalib tells the same story this way: "A free person does not hide the truth; I am 'half a Muslim,' free from the bonds of convention and every religion; and in the same way, I have freed myself from grief at the sting of men's tongues."

In his last years, Ghalib wrote a new Persian dictionary, challenging many traditional etymologies of the old standard dictionary. He said, "You will find that what I have to say about the construction of Persian words and the flights of meaning in Persian verse is usually at variance with what the general run of people say; and I am in the right."

By 1862, Ghalib began to suffer chronic illness off and on, but he continued his voluminous correspondence and his writing. On 15 February 1869, at age 73, Ghalib—

Asadullah Khan Ghalib, known as Mirza Nosha Sahib, died. Hali reports these verses from him:

> Nobody buys my poetry's liquor today, so it sits ageing on
>   the shelf.
> Matured, it will disturb the hearts of devotees not yet born.

> My destiny peaked before I was born.
> The world will applaud my poetry long after I'm gone.

One recurring metaphor that may seem uncomfortable to Western readers is Ghalib's depiction of God as "the beloved," whom he longs for but is rebuffed, betrayed, belittled. By this poetic device Ghalib transforms the "holy" quest for God into an intimate heart-searing relationship. For Ghalib, God is a flirt, not to be trusted.

Ghalib's skill at tight two-liners approached Alexander Pope's for devastating irony. The Urdu ghazal form is based on couplets, but each couplet stands by itself; it has no narrative or logical connection to other couplets in the same ghazal. In Urdu, the first couplet rhymes (AA), and following couplets (usually four to nine in all) use the same rhyme in their second lines only (BA, CA, DA, etc.). I have kept the couplet form, but I have made no attempt to adhere to a rhyme scheme. In a few instances, I have joined isolated but thematically related popular couplets to create ghazals; in each case, the translations are entirely from Ghalib.

Sasha Newborn
Santa Barbara, 2000

SPRING

Who has appeared, God? Whose amazing signs have
          I seen?
The mirror is now a six-layered principle of lingering.

.

When space is scarce, a speck of dust becomes a whole
          mist of longing;
with this net, the vast desert itself is the prey.

.

Dew sprinkles water mirrors on the flower-branch;
nightingale, it's time for spring to be gone.

.

Don't go barefaced to the valley of Majnoon, the mad
          lover.
Every speck of dust hides an impatient heart.

.

O nightingale! Gather a fistful of twigs for a nest
for the first spring storm.

.

Spring is a short season. So what? Spring is here!
Sing of the greening earth and its brisk gusts.

.

The fair one is cruel. What of it? She is loved!
Speak of her grace and her lissom presence.

.

Her beauty I praised, with fine words I described her—
no wonder my confidant has become my rival.

.

Wonderful blessing! she has visited my house!
I look at her, I look at the house!

.

Whoever sits in the shadow of the beloved's wall
is ruler of all India.

.

Fall or spring, the seasons are all alike for me
in my cage, sorrowing over my clipped wings.

.

Spring, recently trapped in buds, now bathes the
        whole town;
Beauty shows its marvels best by peeling out of a
        tightfitting dress.

.

To see the garden, and yearn to pick flowers—
oh Spring-maker, we fall to temptation.

.

Rustic beauty is raped when simple rose-buds are brought
out of the garden and placed in pots in the market.

.

The beloved becomes reluctant when I enter the garden.
If only I didn't love the thrush's song so ardently.

.

The labyrinth of the mind is lit up by bursting seeds.
Imagination sways, our cups are filled again.

.

Can one's eyes possibly see beauty's glow
when springtime overshadows it?

.

THE BELOVED

She walks like an arrow shot from a bow;
how might one find a place in the heart of such a one?

.

With every word, she wants to cut off the speaker's
                    tongue,
so that she might speak, and the other listen.

.

I don't know why I'm chattering on; it's madness.
I hope to God no one understands.

.

Look at what Khizr did to Alexander, after all!
Whom can one turn to for guidance?

.

Ghalib! When all hope is gone,
why complain about anybody?

.

Why should my murderer fear me? What can she
	have on her conscience?
My blood? But that's been flowing freely out of my wet
	eyes all my life.

.

Tormentor, you'll lose your height advantage if
those curls piled on top of your head are unpinned and
	fall down!

.

If another lover needs to write a letter to her, let me
	write it.
Even as dawn broke, I leave my house with a pen behind
	my ear.

.

Dying and living are the same thing if you're in love—
when I see that unfaithful hussy for whom I die, then I
	live.

.

So, is this the tavern door, Ghalib? But where's the
	preachy fellow?
I know this—yesterday he went inside just as I was going
	out.

.

Don't listen if somebody gossips about you;
don't complain if they behave badly.

.

I won't say a word against you, friend, but the next time
          you see
the fellow that you allowed to read my letter, well,
          tell him hello.

.

Every time I open my mouth, you ask me what I am.
Now, honestly, is that any way to speak to me?

.

My pottery cup is better than the cup of Jamshed.
When it breaks, I buy a new one in a shop.

.

I'm not concerned that you're doing pretty well.
When I need a life and a heart, I'll go shopping for them.

.

I mean her style and grace, but I can't speak of them
without also speaking of her stabbing retorts.

.

I speak of creation, but I can't talk of it
except in terms of glasses of wine making the senses reel.

.

Now I've fallen out of grace—but yesterday
when an angel was rude, You condemned it!

.

Tyranny is precious to me; I'm important to the tyrant.
She isn't cruel, except when she's being benevolent.

.

If you couldn't be reached, things would be simpler.
But the truth is, it's not hard to find you.

.

LONGING

N ot every task can be easy,
nor every human attain humanity.

.

Such mad longing—every instant I lean toward her,
will myself to go, and, once there, amazed that I'm all by
      myself.

.

Since appearance demands to be seen,
the mirror itself wants to replace eyelashes.

.

I died scarred by disappointment;
now there you are—like an orchard blooming in a
      hundred colors.

.

She swore she wouldn't torment me—after teasing me to
      death.
O yes, now she's quick to unsay those words!

.

Unfortunately, we never became intimate.
As long as I live, I'll still be waiting.

.

Don't believe me if I say I trust what you promised me.
If I believed it, I would die of joy.

.

If the anguish you profess were a spark struck from a rock,
the rockvein would have bled without stopping.

.

Who can see you? You are unique, one of a kind;
there's not a whiff of anyone like you anywhere, or else I
would have met them.

.

Such mysticism, Ghalib! And such explanations!
People might have mistaken you for a sage, if you weren't
such a drunk.

Ⅰf she ever changes her mind, and is about to be good
          to me,
she remembers her former heartlessness, and backs off.

                           .

He is inattentive to the long story of my lovesickness!
I should be brief; even the messenger is bored.

                           .

As for her, she doesn't trust me, and for my part, I'm
          weak-willed.
She can't ask, and I can't speak.

                           .

I've got to pull myself together, and not despair! What
          kind of heartache is this?
I'm beginning to lose the thread of thinking about my
          love.

                           .

Let me be direct. She only shows herself infrequently,
but for her to be seen at all is more than I can bear.

                           .

O foolish heart! What is the matter with you?
After all, what medicine is there for this pain?

       .

We are eager and she is cold.
O God, what a business this is!

       .

I also have a tongue in my head.
If only she would turn to me to ask what I want!

       .

I sacrifice my life for you.
I don't know how to utter a prayer simply.

       .

I agree that Ghalib is worthless.
But you got him for nothing, so why complain?

       .

While dreaming, you and I made passionate love—
when I awoke, we were no closer and no further apart
than before.

.

I could buy some dreams from sleeping Destiny,
but how much would I have to pay for them?

.

So now I can only bewail the dream-scene that is gone.
You smashed this heart, this many-faceted magnificent
jewel.

.

My destiny peaked before I was born.
The world will applaud my poetry long after I'm gone.

.

Seekers, I didn't want to be mocked for failing.
When I failed to find God, my Self was lost, and I came
back.

.

Your persistent coldness has finally become a glance,
a look that still can't be called face to face.

.

Pretending not to know her lover only gives away the
    beloved.
So, shouldn't she give up turning her face away?

.

You're upset at your own reflection in a mirror.
What if there were more just like you in town, then?

.

How come I didn't suffer burns from the shine of the
    beloved's face?
Now I smolder with anger because my strong eyes
    withstood her frown.

.

Her sarcasm has alienated other guys too.
Look, how contrary she is toward me!

.

For me to dissolve in tears of being apart
is nothing more than a cloudburst for me.

.

I'll keep writing letters even though I have nothing to say
because I love to write your name.

NATURE

The drop is happy to lose itself in the river;
unbearable pain turns into a cure for itself.

.

I am weak—my tears turn into cold breath.
It seems that water can turn into air.

.

Spring clouds break up after heavy rain, as if they
wept so hard that finally they simply disintegrate.

.

Behold the miracle of the scouring winds—
observe the mirror become green in springtime.

.

The rose in bloom prompts us to look and enjoy, Ghalib!
However situations may be colored, keep your eyes open.

.

Everyone accepts you as unique;
no statue, no mirror can do justice to you.

.

The unspoken complaint leaves a mark on the heart;
a drop that never reaches the river simply feeds the dust.

.

If I don't cry drops of blood when a story is told,
then it's not about love, it's just a shaggy dog story.

.

If the eye doesn't see the whole Tigris in one drop of its
          water,
then it's a child's eye merely, and not the inner eye.

.

I know the truth about Paradise, and yet
even so the idea is beguiling.

.

You filled this grand bazaar of a world with dazzlingly
        beautiful sights,
but I suffer bitter pangs—first, my heart is burning, and
        second, my self.

.

I know that I'm a bright candle with its flame always
        searching;
I have no goal, not even a direction; I throw my light
        here and there, with no goal and no rest.

.

Warmed by the stimulation of my imagination, I sing.
I'm a thrush in a garden that doesn't exist.

.

Why else would I value Paradise
than for the fragrant bouquet of red wine?

.

Paradise should be combined with Hell
so that we may be dutiful and also attached to wine and
        honey.

.

I believe in fasting, Ghalib, but
first let me find a reed mat and ice water.

LOVESICKNESS

Where is the exhilaration of wine-filled nights?
Wake up now! The luxury of sleeping late is over.

.

My dust hovers around my love's street;
but now, wind, it has no desire to blow away.

.

Notice the charm of her graceful footprints!
The lilt of her walking has left behind beautiful flowers.

.

Every lusty man worships beauty as his way of life;
now, discriminating taste is not honored.

.

The act of seeing in itself became a veil over the face;
in my rapture, sight just shimmers around your silhouette.

.

How dare you complain? Your heart's been given away.
If the chest has no heart, why should the mouth have a tongue?

.

She won't give up her manners; why should I change mine?
Why be undignified, and ask her what's the matter?

.

Wine makes the heart glad. No matter who holds the glass,
all the muscles of the hand turn into a main artery.

.

My friend knew of my yearning; it gives him heartache. I don't need sympathy.
Why should someone who can't bear my grief share my secrets?

.

Don't be afraid, friend; I'm caged. Go ahead and tell me about the garden.
That nest hit by lightning yesterday—could it be mine?

.

This torment over you is enough to devastate one's home;
why must those who befriend you also have the sky as an enemy?

.

In holy madness, you forfeit nothing; if your house is
          burned, you don't care.
Wasteland is cheap in exchange for an acre of ground.

.

This is indeed a wilderness!
When I see the tangle, I think of home.

.

How can you explain the fire in the heart of imagination?
I thought I was mad when I saw the desert blasted!

.

Is there anybody who has no needs?
If so, how could anyone else help them?

.

Seeing your house again reminds me of the times
I'd bang my head on the wall as if I were mad.

.

Whose costume does this picture poke fun at?
Every face in the painting wears formal dress.

.

Don't ask: My feet are on fire, jail's oppression melts and
        changes.
Here, links of a chain are tempered curls of hair in
        geometric progression.

.

The desperate peacock confuses his victim with illusion.
The garden catches you in its marvelous surroundings by
        its greenness.

.

I'm rapturous; the beloved makes sport of me, and fills
        me with an intense urge to die.
The victim's foot cut off by the beloved's sword is in the
        furnace.

.

Oh, work, oh the agony of living, ah! Don't ask about
        loneliness!
Just to go from morning to evening is like digging the
        Grand Canal.

.

The brick, the hod, the scaffolding, the implements of
        dismantling—
when has a blueprint ever satisfied the construction of
        a life?

.

Why does everybody stare at the wounds of my
        heart?
Let there be no curse on the sturdy arm of my beloved!

.

I can no more forget the color of your hand
than I could tear out a fingernail from mine.

.

When I asked her to verify her promise to behead me,
she smiled and said, "I swear it, by your head."

.

Today I go to my beloved with an axe and a body-bag.
What reason can she give now for not beheading me?

.

Who wouldn't give up their life for the beloved's
        innocence?
She doesn't have any sword in hand, but still she fights!

.

The clouds at sunset remind me of how
the rose garden blazed out when you left.

.

The extinguished candle releases curls of smoke.
        Love's fire
wore dark clothes after I had gone.

.

Skies turn and years go by until the fellow whose heart is
            burning
seems to have come from a fire-breathing family.

.

Mascara is smoke from the fire of
her eyes, their mute expressiveness.

.

In silence I hide a million hopes. I'm an exhausted lantern
in the silent potter's field.

.

The pine and cypress will walk beside you like
   shadows,
if you enter the orchard with this irresistibility.

.

Proof positive of the value of crying is that
pieces of the heart squeeze through the eyes as tears of
   blood.

.

Commanded by the eye, the magical eye,
the mirror, like a parrot, may reply as it is taught.

.

Keeping secrets makes my chest into a furnace;
but if any of them came to light, they might never
   happen.

.

Just think of it as part of the magic treasure of language,
any word that occurs in my ghazals.

.

With every step, I can see how far the goal is from
       me;
at this speed, the desert runs ahead faster than I do.

.

Alone at night, with a relentless fire in my heart,
the shadow slipped away like smoke.

.

The blisters lit up my mad way
through the desert like a string of pearls.

.

Because of you the moving goblet shines in a hundred
              colors;
and this vision is caught in a single, astonished eye because
       of me.

.

From my burning eye, a fire licks out, Ghalib!
The garden soil and dry leaves light up because I look.

.

So, what I have is not love but madness;
then let my madness create your reputation.

.

Don't cut me off completely;
if nothing else, let there be loathing.

.

Though life seems like a lightning flash,
make room only for the heart's passion.

.

I'll make devotion my practice,
though your style is disdain.

.

Ghalib! Keep up your love skirmishes toward her.
If you never actually meet her, then longing must suffice.

.

Because of my drunkenness, I've lost my status;
the drunker I got, the more unreliable I became.

.

A snare had been laid right by the nest;
I didn't even get to fly, and I was captured.

.

Don't ask for news from the lovesick.
Gradually they have turned into grief itself.

.

Sorry night darkens in my gloomy booth.
No sign of daybreak, the last candles gutter out; all is
        quiet.

.

I kept on writing heartbreaking poems in blood,
and, even as I wrote, my hands were cut off.

.

Night is now a golden brandy for me, and heart serves
        the liquor.
I'm drunk on intuition, my imagination a peaceful bar.

.

Ghalib! I didn't give up my sense of humor even while
        begging;
when I became a beggar, I came to love the gentle and
        sympathetic.

.

THE WORLD

The world is simply a face of the Beloved;
if Beauty hadn't wanted to see itself, we wouldn't exist.

.

Every particular place and moment sings pointlessly of its
existence.
Absurdity is the mirror that shows the difference between
madness and sanity.

.

The claim of science is weak and the power of religion
unknown;
Worldliness and Faith are tea leaves at the bottom of the
cup of lethargy.

.

Where the Guardian's footprint is seen,
that dust proves the purity of two worlds.

.

Earth holds center stage by its smugness,
as if the sky always bends down to greet the earth.

If the seer, the seen and sight itself is all the same
        thing,
then where is it exactly, please tell me, that seeing comes
        in?

.

The ocean is thus wave upon wave of forms showing
        themselves,
or, if it isn't, what's the point of these drops and waves
        and bubbles?

.

Every part of the cosmos creaks toward chaos.
The sun flares up like a windblown lantern.

.

Seeking mutters about the restrictions of the heart,
all the turmoil of the river washes by the oyster making a
        pearl.

.

Purity can't show itself without impurities,
this garden is like silver flakes off the mirror of a spring
        breeze.

.

Ghalib, keep firmly in mind the thread of
        Non-existence,
for it holds together the blowing leaves of Existence.

.

Mosque and church mirror this insistent yearning:
the flagging spirit builds shelters to hide in.

.

Ghalib now resides in the shadow of a mosque.
So now, this humble fellow is God's neighbor.

.

We are created, but our independence and self-respect
        make us
turn away at once if the door of the holy Ka'aba is closed.

.

I love past all limits of understanding.
The Ka'aba we see is just a symbol of the real Ka'aba.

.

O Asad, don't be misled by things as they are;
the entire world is caught in the web of thought.

.

When nothing was, God was there, and if I hadn't
    existed, I would have been God.
Yes, existence is my undoing. If I'd never been born, ah,
    what I should have been!

.

The world to me is a children's playground,
the show goes on before me night and day.

.

The absence of absence is called reality.
We woke in our sleep, but we're still dreaming.

.

God, where is your second stage of longing?
All existing possibilities is only one footprint.

.

So, Ghalib, Being is not, and non-Being is not.
What, then, are you yourself, O "Is-not"?

.

As angels record us, we are guilty. What justice is
       that?
Weren't there humans to witness what we did, what they
       wrote?

.

I'm humiliated today, but why? Only yesterday You
       wouldn't allow
an angel to show arrogance toward my nobility.

.

The skies turn across heaven day and night.
Something is bound to happen, so why should I worry?

.

Khizr, we're alive, the ones who understand the busy
       human world are alive,
But not you—you crept away secretly to steal immortality.

.

Prayer beads and the thread that holds them together are
       both fragile,
the best in politics or religion is their strong loyalty.

.

Hurricanes of joy cast wave after wave—of flowers,
of day's end, of winds, of wine.

.

If nothing exists without You, then, O God,
what is all this commotion?

.

What are those bewitching fairies like?
Nods, winks, flirtation—what is all this?

.

Why these twisting, ambergris-perfumed locks?
Why a glance from those eyes shaded with collyrium?

.

Where have the garden and the rose come from?
What is a cloud? What is the wind?

.

"Indeed, if you do good, you will profit from it."
What else is the cry of the dervish?

.

You gave me the two worlds, thinking that would
        make me happy.
As for me, I was doubtful but didn't quibble.

.

What do I care about the son of Mary?
There's always someone who can heal my wounds.

.

I go along for a while with every fast walker I see.
So far I haven't met a single one that's a trusty guide.

.

Following the crowd leads you astray.
That's why I don't follow the caravan's path.

.

The river of sins has dried up, and
it had barely touched the hem of my coat.

.

My friends, you could never cure my rapture.
Even in prison my thoughts ranged as wide as the desert.

.

What's the point of being an iconoclast, and a good
        one,
if my whole life long there's always another rock blocking
        my path?

                        .

Blisters on my feet had panicked me, but
seeing this thorny path has lightened my heart.

                        .

I don't have to take the path Khizr points out—
it'll look like the old guy is keeping me company if I go
        that way.

                        .

My passion makes me dash headlong into an untravelled
        wasteland
guided only by a flirting eye in a picture.

                        .

At every stop along the way, some chose to stay.
But what choice did they have, if they didn't find the
        Way?

                        .

RIVAL

Your other suitor walks around with your letter
        displayed openly,
so that he's forced to show it if someone were to ask.

.

Although she's friendly, her cultivated compassion makes
        me
afraid to touch her even if she were to let me come that
        close.

.

Death is certain; it will come whether or not I wait for it.
But what about my love for you? If you don't come, I
        can't send for you anyway.

.

Who's to say whose vision this is?
You have placed a curtain between us that I can't lift.

.

Ghalib! I have no power over love;
it's a fire I can't light, nor can I put it out.

.

He's lost his heart to her, well, he's human; what can you say?
Even as your rival, he's still your messenger; what can be said?

.

Death positively will not come today, but will come for certain;
I can't tell you how many times I've complained about death.

.

She is careful to ask after me only in public,
knowing that I won't go into detail in a public place.

.

Whenever I plead with her, she says I'm mad. Why bother?
I'm not interested in her answer. What do we have to say?

.

Who says Ghalib isn't bad? But, after saying
that he's distracted, what else is there to say?

.

I too remember all sorts of gay festivities—
but now they decorate the shelf of oblivion.

.

Having all these rivals galls me, unlike Zuleika, Potiphar's
    wife, who was flattered
that other Egyptian women also swooned over Joseph,
    the Moon of Canaan.

.

Let blood stream from my eyes, for tonight we are
    separated.
I'll imagine them to be two burning candles.

.

I'll be revenged on all these beauties in Paradise,
if they become servants there.

.

God, why do her glances strike my heart—
glances that, because of my illness, are indirect.

.

Sighs well up in my chest, but I suppress them.
They are stitching together my torn attention.

.

I went to my beloved's house, but how could I answer
       her jibes?
I'd used up every retort I knew on the butler.

                          .

What is belief? Where is love? If, then, I've chosen to split
       open my head,
O stoneheart, why do you think I picked your porch?

                          .

How can you say that you're not in my heart? Tell me
       this:
When you fill my heart, why don't you fill my eyes?

                          .

You complain unjustly of my heart's absorption in you.
       Whose fault is that?
If you didn't pull away from me, there wouldn't be any
       tension.

                          .

If you're just teasing, what do you do for torture?
Now that you've taken up with my rival, why tease me at
       all?

                          .

What's the point of sarcasm, Ghalib?
Calling her heartless won't make her love you.

The beloved's beauty and her self-esteem have spared
the greedy rival his shame.
She is confident of herself. Why should she test the rival?

.

We agree not to speak—she because of pride in her honor,
and me out of modest consideration for my self-
respect.
How could I meet her on the road? How could she invite
me to her party?

.

Indeed, she has no concern for God. I agree, she is
faithless certainly.
Anyone who values their religion and their heart should
not go to the beloved's lane.

.

I hope she will be faithful
she who does not know what faith is.

.

Nothing will end just because weary Ghalib is no longer
there.
So why do you weep bitterly? Why do you sigh so deeply?

.

J ust knowing that you tease everybody keeps me a
         prisoner to jealousy.
How I wish that you'd flirt only with me!

                              .

From now on, I'll pray to be a long way from the
         beloved, because
it always seems that when I ask for something, the
         opposite occurs

                              .

Jealousy keeps me from even thinking of calling at your
         house.
That's why I've been asking everybody where else to go.

                              .

The smell of roses, a heart-felt cry, smoke from a lamp—
the fellow who left your party early was upset.

                              .

True, I kept away from that impertinent bitch and showed
         my annoyance,
but that pretended display was itself just another phase of
         the madness of love.

                              .

Ah, how charming is his talk!
I feel that what he said was in my heart too.

.

If an acquaintance gives advice, that's not friendship;
they'd better be a doctor or a psychologist.

.

Let's just see what advantage lovers get from their
        beloveds.
A preacher has predicted that this will be a year of hope.

.

You play merely a dusty child's game with Hope;
I see Despair's mocking laughter everywhere, the two
        worlds are its lips.

.

I'll write it down in my book of Deeds.
In the beginning, you wrote out a Word.

.

POETRY

At the Shah's banquet, poetry has begun.
God, keep the door open for these strings of pearls.

.

It's night. The sparkling scene of stars opens again
like the spreading stately doors of a temple.

.

Though I don't understand her words, though I can't
       figure her out,
at least the angelic one has spoken to me.

.

Why is night so dark? Why are sorrows settling in?
Will the stars keep their fixed stare?

.

How can I be happy in a distant city, when even
the letter brought from home has been opened?

.

J ust a few are reborn in rose or tulip;
how many beautiful faces must be hidden in the dust!

.

The Pleiades hide behind day's curtain;
what got into them that they come out naked at night?

.

Was this a garden when I came? Well, a school has
        opened.
The thrushes, hearing my melancholy poems, began to
        recite ghazals.

.

He owns the nights, restful sleep comes for him
on whose arm your hair is strewn.

.

I'm a believer in one God. That's how I can give up all
        rituals;
when differences of doctrine disappear, we become part of
        the all.

.

If Ghalib goes on crying like this, every earthling
will see these cities turn into a wasteland.

.

Reader, hear the echoes of my lament, which I have
    put into these ragged couplets.
In the poetry written on this paper is the lifelong story of
    my tormented heart.

.

My anger and grief is on every bare page, in soiled
    metaphors
that beg for mercy through the vast passageways of
    eternity.

.

We don't know what's in another's heart.
In this world, every person is a page that's never been
    read.

.

I'm not after fame, and I don't write for money.
If my poems are pointless, then so be it.

.

Love has rendered Ghalib unfit for anything else;
in some other world, he too might have been a useful
    fellow.

.

My heart is a fire-temple full of hidden mysteries;
but none of this comes out when I speak.

.

Every word that appears in my poems
is a treasure of appearances full of meaning.

.

Although poetry is a treasure chest of jewels,
intelligence has a gleam of its own.

.

Reason always shows itself new,
so that the eye gives new light to the heart.

.

The treasure that human intelligence can give
to this wild world could make it an enchanted land.

.

When I sell my poems, I'm also selling myself—
but only after taking the measure of the buyer's guile.

.

God, they never understood me and they never will.
Rather than giving me another tongue to better recite my
        poems, why not give them other hearts to hear
        them?

.

So, my poetry is complex! Whenever they hear it,
        academic poets
ask me to write more simply. Well, that's tough, or—it's
        tough stuff!

.

FLUSTERED

How fortunate I am—I envy myself
for just seeing her. How can I bear it?

.

If my anxiety is so intensely hot, I must give myself up to
        a suffering heart:
The wineglass almost melts from the heat of the wine.

.

Lord, how can she stop anyone from being insolent!
She's reluctant to speak up even if the insults shame her.

.

Now, my impatience nags me every moment;
my heart is in such a state that it gets flustered if I just
        stop for breath.

.

Ghalib! My shadow runs away from me like smoke
from my soul on fire; who, then, can stay by me?

.

W hy didn't I burn up when I first saw the lover's
        glowing face?
When I can stare unblinking at such splendor, I burn.

.

People call me a fire-worshipper
because my grumbling throws sparks.

.

The wine bottle tests many;
when you walk by, the wine trembles.

.

We sell ourselves at the price of poetry,
after glimpsing the real intention of the buyer.

.

Bright lightning should have struck us, not Mount Sinai;
wine should be given only after trying the mettle of the
        drinker.

.

I'm neither a song flowering nor the resonance of an
        instrument;
I'm the sound of my own downfall.

       ·

You are absorbed in brushing your curls,
while drawn-out difficulties occupy me.

       ·

We claim self-mastery, but our simple heart is just fooling
        itself.
Actually, we hide our secrets behind an affable disposition.

       ·

Now that you've come, be satisfied with the forehead that
        touches
the ground in prayer.

       ·

It's no wonder that you ask for me now.
I'm miserable, and you look after the pitiful.

       ·

The lightning heat of heart's anguish charged the
        clouds
with high emotion last night; each swirl of the fog was
        liquid flame.

                                    .

A garden of lamps bloomed by the water with a rosy
        luster,
but here a rivulet of blood flowed from teary eye.

                                    .

Headachy and sleepless, I looked for a wall to lean against,
while her beautyship was deep in peaceful sleep, head on
        silken pillow.

                                    .

Where my breath had lit the lamp of forgetfulness,
the splendor of the rose prolonged a friendly meeting.

                                    .

From the earth to the sky was a tumult of color, wave on
        wave.
To me, this vastness was just a door to a burning waste

                                    .

Then suddenly the heart, ravished with the joys
of pain, began to drip red tears of blood.

                                    .

The heart was enraptured when the storm came, but
the lover's soul was only a reed in crashing waves and
        pouring rain.

                                    .

THE SPECTATOR

The mind's dealer shuffles our circumstances like
        cards,
and we change like turning pages in a book.

.

The world seems so small to me, and
the sky no bigger than an ant's egg!

.

In their grieving household, liberated people
mourn for no more than a moment, like lightning
        flashing.

.

I'm still learning lessons at the college of sorrow:
how to say the words "gone" and "was."

.

Ghalib died a long time ago, but we can't forget
how he'd so often ask: What if it had been otherwise?

.

An intelligence indifferent to the world circles back
        on itself in despair
but the mirror of the world traps a person's reflections.

.

You spend your life admiring yourself in the mirror of life
        in a hundred colors, and
this spectator is confounded by the alternation of night
        with day.

.

God, your title of The One is truly well-founded.
Even a beauty facing You with the smoothest brow
        doesn't reflect You.

.

If I'd been even higher up, I might have seen
        everything—
if only I could have sat above and behind God's throne.

.

What is the awe-struck spectator waiting for, God?
Everything we anticipate is a mirror of our world.

.

He feels despair about nonexistence when he hears the
        roar of the stadium crowd.
Asad, one's eyes aren't just a gleam in philosophy's
        mirror.

.

To me this world is like children playing games.
The show unfolds in front of me day and night.

.

A child's playing is for me like the throne of Solomon;
any trifle can be a miracle in my eyes.

.

You'd see the way the conversation would flow
if you'd just let someone put a glass and wine jug before
      me.

.

Let this be the last bloody ocean of storms!
But still I anticipate an as yet unknown flood.

.

If indecisiveness pulls me apart, faith props me up;
Mecca's behind me, church dogma is up ahead.

.

Though my hands are numb, at least my eyes are alive;
leave the wine jug and glass right here in front of me.

.

He's a friend, a good fellow in every way:
Why do you badmouth Ghalib when he's standing right
      here?

.

Newcomers, beware the chamber of desires!
You may hunger and thirst away your lives.

.

Watch me if your eyes are sharp enough to see a warning.
Listen, if you can hear advice.

.

The waitress in her beauty defies faith and reason;
the player's songs rob you of intelligence and calm.

.

So, at night we look around at this corner of pleasure;
it's a gardener's shelf, or a florist's tray.

.

Watching the waitress walk, listening to the guitar
one thrills the eyes, the other the ears.

.

Ah, but if you come back here in the morning,
you won't find last night's euphoria, no music, no
        bubbling laughter.

.

Burned-out at the disbanding of last night's party,
a candle stands, its flame also gone.

.

These ideas come to me out of the sky.
Ghalib, the pen's scratching is a hymn.

.

DEGRADATION

In the company of her friends, I have no shame;
I just sat, even when fingers pointed at me.

.

I pawned my ragged coat and my prayer rug to buy a jug
of wine;
it's been a long time since I drank together with the wind
and rain.

.

If it were my lot, I'd ask the earth; You miser!
What do you do with the invaluable treasures that we
bury?

.

Surely she picked up this new habit elsewhere;
she's started giving kisses without being asked.

.

Stubbornness is another matter. Except for that, she's not
really bad;
often, she's kept promises that she forgot she made.

.

I've had a thousand desires, and each one
    heart-stopping.
Much has been granted me, yet even those have not been
    enough.

.

We've always been told of Adam's fall from Paradise,
but I was more humiliated when I left your
    neighborhood.

.

Drunkenness and I have been much together these past
    years;
wine-king Jamshed's foretelling cup should come once
    more.

.

I wanted a friend to confide my love-weariness to,
but he wearied of the tartness of depression sooner than I
    did.

.

Preacher! For God's sake, don't peek behind the Ka'aba's
    curtain.
You might find the same doubting image I did.

.

My heart isn't made of brickwork; why shouldn't it fill with pain?
A thousand times I cry; why does the beloved make us weep?

.

I'm not sitting in the temple or the mosque, not at the window or on the doorsill.
I'm sitting on a public road. How can anyone make us get up from here?

.

When the beauty that dazzles the midday sun itself burns your eyes,
why does she hide her face under a veil?

.

Your glance is a dagger which cuts deeply, a flirting arrow from which there is no refuge
how could the very reflection of your face in the mirror dare to confront you?

.

The prison of life and the chains of grief are in fact the same thing.
How might someone find escape from grief before death?

.

Ghalib has endured every possible trouble.
There's only one matter left to come—a quick death.

.

Dressed as a beggar, Ghalib, I observe
the behavior of the liberal citizens.

.

The beloved mistook me for a beggar, and didn't say
        anything.
But—curse my foolish luck—I fell at the feet of the guard.

.

Ha! I laugh at every humiliation she dumps on me.
It's convenient that her night watchman is an
        acquaintance of mine.

.

Don't think that my wailing disrupts anything at my
        beloved's party,
because they welcome my laments like a sad song there.

.

I was no scholar, nor was I master of any discipline.
There's no reason why, then, heaven turned against me.

.

When I was alive they'd throw me out of the meeting.
Now that I'm nearly dead, let's see who carries me out.

.

DISAPPOINTMENT

I leave, carrying the scars of my regret at not having
    lived in better times;
I'm blown out, like a candle, no longer fit for company.

.

The mirror opens to the six senses;
so, the perfect and the flawed aren't separate.

.

Yearning has unbuttoned the dress that hid Beauty;
nothing is between us except for seeing.

.

Loyalty has died in my heart because
it is not rewarded, but only tantalized by hope.

.

I'm not afraid of love's treachery, but, Ghalib,
recall this once-proud heart.

.

You should have paused for me.
Now you've gone on, so linger there a little.

.

Over your shoulder, you said the next time we met would
        be a cold day in hell,
as if hell were somewhere far away.

.

In my house, you were like a full moon.
Couldn't things have stayed that way a little longer?

.

True, you hated me and didn't get along with Nayyar,
you wouldn't even linger to watch your children play.

.

Fools! Don't wonder that Ghalib still lives.
It's my fate to be alive, yet long for death.

.

W ings are so light that even the wind can lift them.
Without wind, these feathers have no strength or
    endurance.

.

A heavenly era is coming now
and the whole spotless path seems like a flower show.

.

Drinkers are drunk simply with the idea of the appearance
    of the rose,
for there's nothing else intoxicating in the walls or door
    of the wine cellar.

.

I'm ashamed by my own ruinous love;
this house has nothing but the regret of failing to achieve.

.

So, Ghalib, my verses are just a pleasant hobby;
obviously, I gain nothing by displaying my talent.

.

Ifyou couldn't bear the frustration of disappointment,
then why on earth did you want to share my sorrow?

.

I might throw up a smokescreen to hide my bad
            reputation,
but love is spared no embarrassment around you.

.

The dignity that love promised has gone underfoot;
too bad! Trustworthiness is gone from this world.

.

The ear is cut off from words and the eye denied vision.
A heart responds—but it is waterlogged with sorrow!

.

Ghalib! this love hasn't been colored by insanity;
even the perverse desire to be known as wretched is
            frustrated.

.

Heart, how precious is this grief and sorrow;
     someday
you won't sigh at midnight nor cry until morning.

.

I know that grieving constantly is fatal, but my heart can't
     stop.
If I weren't lamenting for love, I'd still cry for the world.

.

A life sentence and the sentence of grief amount to the
     same thing.
So, what's the point of finding salvation before dying?

.

Don't call me in to the rose garden when I'm sad and
     lonely.
I can't bear to look at the flowers smiling.

.

If you knew I was to bear so much pain,
you should have known enough to give me more than
     one heart.

.

The world killed you, Asadullah Khan.
Whatever happened to your passion, your spirit?

.

Even a dewdrop on a red poppy has a meaning—
there's a scar on her unscrupulous heart so that shame
may come.

.

A dove is just a fist of ash, and a nightingale a color
prison;
my complaint, the rind of seared heart, doesn't compare.

.

The flame itself couldn't hurt me as much as the urge to
be burned has;
my heart is sad when spirit fades.

.

You say you're a prisoner of love because you can't
escape—
as a hand caught under a stone must lift, one vows always
to keep a vow.

.

O World-warming Sun! Shine your brilliance this way too;
like a shadow over us, strange times have come.

.

WEAKNESS

Come, love; I get no rest without you;
I'm not strong enough to bear any more waiting.

.

They offer us paradise when we give up earthly life,
but the hangover doesn't measure up to the happiness of
   existence.

.

My tears drive me away from your dinner table;
ah well, I can't control my own tears.

.

My heart no longer sees any point in anything, nor any
   pleasure;
if it weren't for new flowers blossoming, I wouldn't
   notice the spring.

.

Ghalib! You swore you'd never drink again;
but there is no conviction in your promise.

.

The rain gave her an excuse not to show her alleged
        regard for me,
for it kept her from walking over to see me.

                          .

As for me, the rush of my tears created a flood—
with my white cotton pillow a white froth on the
        bubbling waters.

                          .

When I see the beloved, my face lights up,
but she just thinks it means I'm getting better.

                          .

We are like a combination lock—doomed to come apart
just when everything clicks into place.

                          .

The rose scoffs at the thrush's infatuation.
What is called love is simply the mind out of kilter.

                          .

Why would I find life worth more than the beloved?
Haven't I kept true to my beliefs?

                          .

Many tears have made me unafraid, and bold in my
  love.
They've washed me so clean that I no longer hide my
  passion.

.

I've lost all sense of the passage of time;
when you left, I felt the shadow of fate pass by.

.

It wasn't until my lips were injured
that I could even manage to talk with you.

.

You ought to know the depth of bewilderment of
  someone
whose great hope it is to die.

.

Heartless one, give me a new anguish to bear, so that
you may enjoy my embarrassment all the more.

.

It's never clear where the impulse to seek originates.
I'm a tongue that's been cut off, like an ocean wave
        breaking.

                    .

I can't stand even my own longing for her.
I'm dying, but I refuse to ask for her—for fear that I
        might appear demanding.

                    .

I watched in vain until my eyes were shut at last.
When she was finally brought to my bed, I could no
        longer see.

                    .

A kiss might cost my life, but why did she say so now?
She must know that Ghalib is barely half alive.

                    .

How will I ever find a comfortable life and wealth?
Where is everything that I need to rest?

                    .

NOSTALGIA

Simple desire! Yes, just
once more calling to mind her bewitching vision.

.

Life might have gone on as usual.
Why do I remember your path?

.

Again, my mind drifts to your street!
But I remind myself that that is where my heart was lost.

.

What utterly abandoned land this is!
The desert makes me think about my house.

.

In my childhood, Ghalib, I once picked up a stone to
        throw at the Mad Lover;
but as soon as I did, I thought of my own craziness.

.

It's been so long since I played host to her,
a long time since the brimming wineglass lit up our
        evenings.

                    .

My hot breath is throwing sparks of regret again;
we hadn't visited the lights in a long time.

                    .

The heart and the eye, usually enemies, are together
in seeking opportunities to see, and to imagine.

                    .

I want to see her on her balcony again,
her black hair blowing across her face.

                    .

Ah, if I could once more call back those days and nights
        of leisure,
so that I may spend my hours thinking and dreaming of
        love.

                    .

No more do we meet and part!
O, those nights, months, years!

.

Who has time to spend in love!
No more pleasure in seeing Beauty!

.

In one's imagination,
young thoughts come no more!

.

Crying blood doesn't come easily;
that takes a strong heart, steady nerves!

.

Ghalib! My limbs are now weak.
There's no stability in the world!

.

Fire is not as miraculous, nor is lightning as delicate;
so just tell me what that exasperating, capricious one is!

.

The heart must have been burnt up if the body burned.
What are you looking for in these ashes?

.

We do not agree that running through the veins is
        enough;
if it doesn't go through the eyes, it isn't really blood.

.

The reason we look forward to paradise
is the simple promise of musky rosé wine.

.

Now he calls himself a friend of the king, and walks
        around pompously;
except for that, Ghalib has no status in the city.

.

WINE

The tulip and the eglantine have different colors;
whatever the color, we witness the spring.

.

We learn how to draw in order to meet moonfaced
        women;
we need some excuse to get together.

.

What kind of bastard drinks wine for pleasure?
I need to forget something about myself night and day.

.

Let your head rest by the mug on the bar for your hour
        oblivion;
then, at prayer times, turn your face toward Mecca.

.

By which I mean that, even as the facets on the glass of
        life sparkle in turn,
the wise person is always drunk on the wine of themself.

.

Ghalib relishes his poverty with style—
he soaks dry breadcrumbs in wine.

.

After the holiday party of childhood was over,
I spent my teens in days of drinking.

.

How could I possibly return home dry?
Even if I suppress the urge to drink, what's to keep the
        bartender from forcing me?

.

The wind has the same effect as wine.
It makes drinking superfluous.

.

If I ever give up bars, it won't matter where I am—
a mosque, or a college, or even a monastery.

.

Ghalib has sworn off wine, but despite that,
sometimes on a gray day or at night under the moon, he
        drinks.

.

Intoxicated people are heir to six dimensions,
but to the unknowing, the whole world is boring.

.

I hate to tell the bartender, but to tell the truth
I can be satisfied with what's left in my glass.

.

When the river is at flood stage, the banks can't stay dry
        however hard they try.
Likewise, when you're in a bar, you can't stay too
        intelligent.

.

Bartender, if you won't serve me a glass, then let me drink
        out of my hand.
Here, pour me some wine, and I won't even touch a
        glass.

.

Like an eye under its eyebrow,
the tavern ought to be right near the arched mosque.

.

Ghalib has come at last.
Majruh, bring good wine and rose water.

.

Preacher, you don't drink, and you don't offer drinks;
your cellar has spiritual wine indeed!

.

Why do you turn down a cup, saint?
It's wine, not bee vomit (honey).

.

When you drink, wine takes its color from your lips
and the cup watches you with the gardener's lusty eyes.

.

Of course, I borrowed money to buy booze,
but I knew that some day the needs in my life will change.

.

At his meetings, a glass of wine rarely was offered.
So when he hands me a glass, I wonder if the bartender
        has mixed me a mickey.

.

Let your sunshine fall on me, not on Mount Tur.
Wine should be poured in proportion to how much the
        drinker can take.

.

DEATH

The Garden of Eden that the prophet sings about
is just a bunch of flowers in a forgotten corner to
                    someone drunk on ecstasy.

.

In a mirrored hallway, you appear multiplied,
as the sun does reflected by dewdrops.

.

Hidden in my sentences is the shape of ruin—
a farmer's hot blood may discharge suddenly like static
                    while threshing corn.

.

Silence hides a thousand futile dreams;
I'm like the burnt-out lamp on a stranger's grave.

.

Ghalib! The fact of death is always in sight;
it's shared by all this world's scattered pieces.

.

From fear of disgrace, you hid under a blanket of
    dirt—the final barrier to love's secrets!
Who could do more to keep a lover secret? Ah me,
    ah me!

.

You had vowed a marriage for life, but to what end?
Life doesn't last either. Ah me, ah me!

.

How can a fellow endure these dark nights of rain alone
after having watched the slow stars turn, waiting for his
    beloved. Ah me, ah me!

.

Suffering took away my belief in the reality of anything.
Should I claim this as a wound in my heart?

.

I remember the countless scars on my heart from dashed
    hopes.
God, don't ask me for an exact accounting of my deeds.

.

Knowing that death will come gives
meaning and a tang to life's pleasures.

.

Grass grows on my house, on the door and walls.
Too bad I'm so devastated just when spring comes to
            visit.

.

You should reward me, God, for the sins I wanted to
            commit but didn't,
as well as punishing me for the ones I did.

.

When we've lost all hope,
what's the point in complaining about anyone else?

.

A shroud to cover my naked humiliation—
alive, I embarrassed life in every fashion I wore.

.

If I weren't afraid of disgracing my beloved, I'd die
        willingly,
but death hides no secrets.

.

It seems as if no hope will ever be realized, and there's no
        way out.
I used to laugh at my own desperation, but nothing can
        make me smile any more.

.

A day for my death has been settled on;
then why shouldn't I sleep comfortably at night?

.

I long for death, but, even though it's just around the
        corner,
death still eludes me.

.

It's said that humans live on hope,
but I'm downhearted; I don't hope to live.

.

My last breath is dawdling on its way.
O friends, now I see only God.

.

Carrying a rider with no reins, no stirrups,
the horse of the years gallops by, watch where it pauses.

.

Like the shadow of the bridge on floodwaters,
you should dance on the tumbling waves of destiny!

.

I'm not afraid of the Grim Reaper, and I don't argue with
        the Preacher,
I know It, no matter what disguise It comes in.

.

By the time the ship reaches shore,
what's the point of rebelling against the boatman's
        power?

.

The sun shows the dew how to evaporate.
I'm here, too, until I feel the gentle nudge.

.

That which you and I call the bruised sky
is the ancient dissolving altar of the hermit named Ghalib.

.

When a person gets used to suffering, suffering
	disappears.
I've faced so many troubles that now it's easy for me to
	deal with them.

.

Now take me away somewhere where they don't speak my
	language,
and there'll be nobody to sing with me.

.

I'll own a house without any walls, without neighbors,
	with no guard at the door;
no one will care, and when death comes, there'll be no
	mourners there.

.

What right do you have to complain, Ghalib, about
	strangers?
Can't you remember the indifference of your fellow
	nationals?

.

Death came to me in a stranger's house far away from my
	country.
That way God took care of my helplessness and poverty.

.